COME
BACK TO ME

ELIZABETH BODNER

WITH LOUISE DUNN

COME
BACK TO ME

Messages from the God-Self Within
Affirming the Journey of Life

Mill City Press
Minneapolis, MN

MILL CITY PRESS, INC.
212 3ʳᵈ AVENUE NORTH, SUITE 290
MINNEAPOLIS, MN 55401
612.455.2294
WWW.MILLCITYPUBLISHING.COM

ISBN-13: 978-1-936780-78-5
LCCN: 2011934663

COVER DESIGN AND TYPESET BY MELANIE SHELLITO

PRINTED IN THE UNITED STATES OF AMERICA

DEDICATION

To Molly, Brooke, Austin, Bobby, Danny, and
Ricky, my six grandchildren.

You fill my life with love and joy.

NOTE FROM THE AUTHOR

The following messages were received in daily journaling with my God-Self. Sitting at the computer or with my journal each day over many months, I thanked the God-Self and then asked, *Dear Presence, what would you have me be, know, understand, and do?* Then I waited for the guidance. I was amazed at the absolute love that came forth in the writings. I was surprised at the gentle yet firm reminding of who I truly am. There was also obvious humor as I watched God's willingness to work with me, a faithful skeptic.

I see these writings today as a gift and a total affirmation of God's love, and I share them with you in humility and joy.

May they lift your spirit and give you hope in the journey.

Elizabeth Bodner

HOMECOMING

Come home to Me. Honor Me! Stay with Me! Come home to Me and stay here for eternity. Life is fun and joyful when you live it consciously with Me. I am your answer. I am the truth that you seek. I am the joy that you want.

I give you direction to be what you really want to be. I help you know what to do each moment. I am the illumination within your mind. I am the peace and love that you yearn for. I am the clarity and understanding you desire. I am that I am.

I am the all. I am perfection. I am the perfect understanding.

I am everything.

I am here for you!

Oh God,
You are all that I want, all that I long for
this day. Bring me home to You.

PRESENCE

I am the way of truth and happiness. With Me you are never alone. All that is around you might seem to be empty. It is not. Love and light, even in the seeming darkness, surround you. You are not alone. You cannot be alone.

The angels are with you. You feel isolated when you forget them and Me. This isolation is a human creation. Trust Me. I am with you in each moment. Do not wander around in the shadows. The light beckons you always. Darkness turns you away from your path. Look to Me and trust that I am here, in you and with you at all times.

I love you. I answer your every call instantly.

Thank You, God,
let me never forget, even for an instant,
that Your perfect Love
enfolds me.

LISTENING

Listen to Me.

Live in the mystery rather than in the results you would like to have happen. You set the stage and bring all the elements into play, and then the unfolding happens. Visualize harmony and perfection everywhere.

See the God-perfection in everything that you do. You are a light and have great power. The Cosmic Beings are working with you and all the children of light. The angels are with you all the time. You must do your part. I can help you.

You know your calling. Don't be lazy. Do your work. Your work is important. Always feel your perfection and wholeness. Be with Me and listen within to hear and receive My love and direction. I am with you always.

All is in Divine Order.

*In the Stillness of this moment
I hear Your Voice
and listen.*

INNOCENCE

Enjoy what you are experiencing now. Take this one *now* moment and savor it. Drain it of its essence. Do the same with each moment. That is the way to live life.

All is here *now* for you to explore, taste, drink, sample. The more aware you are, the fuller and richer your life becomes. As you are present in the moment, little things appear to delight you. You see the world before you as you have never seen it before and with a new inner knowing about your connection to all. Be like the innocent child and see life for the first time, and embrace it.

Live in the wonder of the moment.

I am awake to the
beauty, majesty, and mystery
of this moment.

CREATION

Be involved in your life! Be alive and interested in activities that feed you and give you pleasure. Be aware! Be active! Create the life you want! You have created much that does not serve you. Now create that which does. The angels will help you if you but ask.

All of Heaven loves you. Remember this. Please love yourself enough to happily do your work. Don't be lazy. Live. Laugh, sing, dance, and play your way through each day!

Celebrate!

Thank!

Praise!

Rejoice!

This is God's way!

*Today I actively and consciously
create the life I want.
God is my Guide in all things.*

JOY

Life is not serious every moment. It is light and joy and fun.

Learn to play more in your life and to explore. The more open you are to living fully, the more options you have to do things differently.

Remember to laugh; laughter removes tension. It is easier to receive blessings when you have dropped the barrier of seriousness. Remember to sing, laugh, dance, and play, as I have said before. Be in the moment and enjoy it fully.

All is in Divine Order.

Here I am, dear God.
Thank You for playing with me today.

CELEBRATION

Celebrate each moment of life. It matters not what seems to be going on around you; celebrate! Life is a celebration. It is a schoolroom on planet Earth. It is an opportunity to come closer to Me. Stay connected to Me at all times. I know what you are trying to achieve in this lifetime.

Do not judge yourself. Be kind to yourself. Serve others. You are a divine being in embryo. Become that fully. This takes you back to Me and off the wheel of birth and death cycles.

Dwell in My Light. Dwell in My abundance. Dwell in the sacredness of life. Dwell in the land of forgiveness. Dwell in the bounty of the Universe. Dwell in My Love.

Be love at all times and in every way. Sow love with your every breath. Manifest your destiny with love, caring, and serving. Love one another.

All is in Divine Love.

Dear God,
You are my one and only home.
Bring me closer to You with every breath
and heartbeat.

KNOWING

You ask, "Who am I?" You are a child of God. You are the Light of everlasting Glory. You are a partner in the creation of your universe and the world. You are like a grain of sand on a beach—seemingly insignificant as a being and yet an integral part of the whole of humanity.

You are a necessary part in the perfection of the Universe. You are a catalyst of change at this time of living, holding the Light for others and accepting your role with joy.

You are everlasting life. You are here and hereafter. You are eternity. You are change. You are the yesterdays and tomorrows and the ever-present NOW.

I am Your perfect creation, oh God.
Help me to know my worth
and worthiness.

HUMILITY

Hear Me and take action.

Forgive! Stop criticizing! Stop complaining and fault-finding. What needs fixing is within you and nowhere else. If you keep focusing on others, you cannot see the inner work which you need to do.

Live the Love and Kindness that you are. Stop focusing on someone or something else. It is about you and no one else. When you feel critical, you are criticizing something within you that is not yet complete. The other person, place, or thing is a catalyst for you to see something to correct within.

Forget the outer and immediately go into the Silence. Go into the God Presence. Ask, and listen for direction. Follow that guidance and walk the path of change. Be humble and admit when you are wrong. Release and surrender whatever needs to be released.

Forgive yourself. Forgiveness is the way to Joy, Peace, and Love.

Divine Spirit,
take my critical thoughts
and replace them
with Your Silence and Your Love.

PRESENCE

Live in the present moment. Each moment is full of everything that is, has been, or will be. Each moment is the ever-present NOW!

Time is a figment of the human mind. You think you live one moment at a time. In reality, past, present, and future are all NOW. Each moment that you live consciously, you are alive. In that moment you create all that you choose to bring into your life.

The moments that you are unconscious, you also create and bring negativity and fear into your life which you then later need to release.

It is easier and more enjoyable creating love, peace, service, joy, and harmony. You create them by living in the ever-present NOW.

There is no past;
there is no future;
there is only now.
And in that now I live fully with You,
dear God.

STILLNESS

Spend time in the quiet with Me and have a conversation.

I am here to help you.

Use Me to safely walk through whatever is being stirred up in your life, no matter which way it is being stirred up in you. This is the moment to release and surrender that which no longer serves. Be aware and do your inner work.

Be in the silence and listen! Guidance comes in the silence.

Clarity comes in the silence; direction comes in the silence. Inner knowing becomes clear to you in the silence.

Renew in the silence. Learn in the silence. Discover choices and options in the silence. Allow, be, wait, discover, and listen in the silence. Embrace life and live in and from the silence.

All is in Divine Order.

Divine Presence,
quiet my busy, chattering mind.
Speak Your Love to me all through this day.

LIFE

Live your magnificence always, every moment. Surrender and release everything human. Trust that all is in Divine Order. You are an integral part of that Order. You *are*, and you know it. Allow all that you are to emerge into each instant of time.

You have work to do. Do your work and do it consciously.

Be joyful and enthusiastic each and every moment. Life is for living fully each moment. Savor the breath, the light, and the expansion every instant. Create your world gleefully; serve others constantly; live compassionately.

Remember what you know. Be all that you are. Lovingly support others on their journey. Allow life to flow freely.

Laugh, dance, sing, and play. Have fun this very day. Live life fully and give it your all!

All is in Divine Order.

Today I play!
I surrender all worry and simply relax
into joy.

AWARENESS

Change your perspective and you change your world and the way you feel about it. Thoughts, feelings, and actions create your world.

Be aware of your thoughts. Be attuned to your feelings. Choose your actions consciously. Be your own advocate. Lobby for your highest good. Stand up for your being.

Open to your inner self and let the guidance come through.

Your inner guidance is getting stronger and you are beginning to hear My Voice. The longer you stay in the silence within yourself, the happier you will be.

Stay connected to Me always. Walk your path. I guide you and help you along the way. Rest assured that all is being done for you that your Highest Self allows.

Today I spend more time in the Silence.
I am renewed; I am content;
I am awake!

CELEBRATION

Celebrate all life, both seen and unseen. Celebrate the weather of the day, the rain and snow showers, the sunshine and the wind.

Celebrate knowing God and reveling in God's love. Celebrate each breath, each moment, each joy, each person, each vibration, each and every opportunity to expand your inner light.

Celebrate every knowing and learning. Celebrate your essence. Celebrate your service to life. Celebrate each lesson that comes your way. Celebrate life in its fullness, including so-called death, which is only a new beginning.

Celebrate beingness.

Celebrate choices.

Celebrate who you are and who you came here to be.

My heart is full of gratitude for the gift of life.
I celebrate the life of God
within each glorious moment.

REVELATION

ALL IS IN DIVINE ORDER!

You are being shown the path that best suits your spiritual aspirations and yearnings. Clearing up mistakes of the past and finishing the present work is imperative.

You are manifesting spiritual connections with others. You are finding activities that bring you joy and happiness. Let your mantra today be: *Nothing is hidden. All I need to know is revealed.*

Do your inner work. Stay away from those things that keep you numb. Be awake! Stay awake! Live awake! Be aware and mindful each moment. Walk the walk of life.

I love you and help you always.

Nothing is hidden;
all that I need to know is revealed.

FREEDOM

You are coming to understand the confusion that clutter brings to your life. It dis-empowers and negates positive feelings you have for yourself. It helps you be lethargic and lose interest in things. It is overwhelming for you.

You are responsible for what you bring into your house. You are responsible for where you put things and how you care for them. You are learning that *less is more* and that is the lesson you are practicing. Give things away that you are no longer using. Go through your clothes, go through shelves, and dispose of those things that are not serving you constructively.

Laugh, dance, sing, and play as you de-clutter your home and your life. Your spirit soars when it is not chained to things. BE FREE! RELEASE!

You are learning to be in control of your home. As you clear up your physical home, your inner home also becomes balanced, because you are taking care of your body, heart, mind, and soul.

*Today I de-clutter
and open my mind to the order
and harmony that is God.
I act responsibly with all material things.*

JOY

You have been struggling with boredom. You have sought remedies which do not satisfy. You hide from the problem; you hide from yourself. You know that when you do this you are not present, you are not truly living, and you merely wait for something to change. It doesn't change, and you know it will *not* until you choose to take control of your life again.

Whenever you feel bored or lonely or any other negative feeling, begin to pray for someone else. Get out of yourself and help another. That is a healing balm for both of you.

Remember that joyful giving in any form brings quick results. Joy is a major part of a fulfilled life. Joy is expansive and spreads the Light of happiness.

Be of good cheer.

God is here.

Take me out of self-absorption today,
dear God,
and help me attend to the needs of others.

DIVINE ORDER

You ask what Divine Order means; here is the answer:

Divine Order is simplicity.

Divine Order is perfection.

Divine Order is love and harmony.

Divine Order allows all to unfold in freedom of choice.

Divine Order encourages.

Divine Order is peace, happiness, and joy.

Divine Order honors everything and creates beauty with only a thought.

Divine Order connects everything to everything else.

All is One.

When you declare Divine Order for your life, you are asking for My help and help is given. You ask for guidance, peace, rest, whatever is needed. I am here for you, with you, and in you.

When you declare Divine Order, you trust that all things are given and all unfolds perfectly, for the good of all.

Today I decree Divine Order
in all areas of my life.
Guidance is given and peace is restored.

EXPANSION

ALL IS HERE NOW! THERE IS NOWHERE ELSE IT CAN BE!

Contemplate the power of this statement.

There are different vibrations of energy. The higher vibrations are here as well as the lower vibrations. You see and feel those that resonate with you. The higher vibrations are in every NOW moment; they are faster and different than those you normally resonate with and can feel.

You are raising your vibration as you do your work and release the things that do not serve your highest good. You are clearing up your emotional, physical, spiritual, and etheric bodies. As you do that, your vibration expands and rises. You are overcoming the human ego and living as the Divine.

You are learning and remembering every day the truth of your being. You will enjoy your life more when you no longer judge and criticize and when you spend more time in the NOW. Living in the moment allows you to taste, savor, experience, and live life more fully.

Divine Order allows!

Divine Timing permits!

Divine Love supports you always!

Here, now, in You
I need nothing but You, my God.

GUIDANCE

Know first of all that you are a child of God and you are never alone. Know that you are love, loving, loved. Understand that you have the tools to create perfection and to alter any imperfection which you have created.

Do what your heart guides you to *do*. Be a loving person who serves others in love. Understand that you are here now to perfect your world. You chose to live on Earth at this time; you chose the lessons you came to learn; you are never a victim, even when you think you are.

You always have help in walking through each day of your life. However, you must ask before the help can be given. That is Divine Law. I, your God, am here for you! I love you and spur you on in your journey.

Be present and awake and do what you know is the right thing to do each and every moment. Listen to your inner guidance and live accordingly.

I am always guided from within.
Help is available to me if I will only ask.

TRUST

Release the ego that struggles, fights, and withdraws into its own power. This is not the truth of you. Holding on to the human ego keeps you captive and on the wheel of confusion and resistance.

Change the way you approach life. Jump off the cliff of uncertainty, in faith, and release all that holds you back. All fear is nothing in this NOW moment; it is but a memory of past experience. Is it really worth holding on to? Are you willing to lose each present moment and live in mere memories?

The choice is yours. Think about this as you go into your daily activities.

All is in Divine Order.

With Your help, dear God,
I let go of fear and uncertainty;
I walk in faith and trust You in all things.

LIGHT

Live life fully, from the fullness of your heart. No longer are you a lost soul. Your being is a light in the darkness. You are found, with a mission to embrace Me fully! Know that each moment you are getting closer to fulfilling the Divine Plan of your life.

You have opened to Me and earnestly yearned to be one with Me. Now in your meditations visualize yourself walking to the Light, leaving behind the ego and all misuse of life energy. Feel my love grow in, through, and around you. Feel it grow deeper than ever before, expanding out from you. Then go about your day of serving others, trusting your relationship with Me.

I am here with you always.

Today my soul expands in the Light.
I feel and know my oneness
with God.

DIRECTION

Continue to connect to Me consciously. Notice the calm you are feeling. Peace, joy, and emptiness fill you. The emptiness is the release of mind chatter and the need to do anything. You are right here, now! You are present in the moment. This is the only place there is.

Always return your mind to peace. Revel in that inner peace, which so easily flows from your times of meditation. Give yourself freely to Me, and let your burdens, thoughts, agendas, and all worldly concerns fall away.

Stay open to receive My direction and then follow it. Notice that your inner world is peaceful and soothing while the busy outer world is filled with noise, confusion, and restlessness.

Be aware. Create your life and your world the way you consciously desire it to be.

You are a co-creator with Me.

Peacefully resting in You, dear God,
I joyfully create a new day.

PERFECTION

All in this world is Divine Timing in Divine Order. All is here, now. All is! Utilize what is and manifest your world of perfection. That means releasing your inner thoughts, feelings, and words of judgment, anger, criticism, hate, or even simple dislike. Focus on the perfection that is within you and within all.

Focus on wholeness rather than lack in any situation. You are connected at all times to the whole. You are what you are, and you have created yourself through your thoughts, feelings, and words. Use different thoughts and you create something else. The same is true with your words and feelings.

Hold the picture of perfection and that is what you create. Living in imperfection creates more of the same. The way you change your world is by being aware of what you are creating each and every moment.

You are a spiritual being having a human experience. Take advantage of each moment.

My love is with you.

This is the moment
and now is the time
for me to live the perfection
of my Divine Self.

ABUNDANCE

Serving others is one way to be joyful in this world. Taking care of oneself is another. Being kind to everything and everyone brings kindness into your world.

Being enthusiastic in each moment keeps you awake and aware. Then you make choices that seem "right" or "best" or "good" for you, rather than merely responding from habit. Life is full of opportunities to be who and what you want to be. You must be aware and choose.

Monitor your thoughts and stop those that are "lack" oriented. There is no lack in the Universe. Thinking from lack draws it to you. Be in charge of your thoughts. What are you thinking right now; and now; and now; and now?

Be aware. Stay conscious and enthusiastic.

Wake up and live!

The full abundance of Creation
fills my mind
and directs my thoughts today.

CHOICE

What do you want to be today? *Who* do you want to be today? *How* will you be that? Do you make your choices with enough conviction to live them all day long? THE CHOICE IS ALWAYS YOURS.

You are choosing the life you want to live every single moment. Choose consciously. Are you living your life intentionally right now, or are you merely going through the motions like a robot?

Think of these things as you go about your day. You always have time to be conscious and aware. You will know what you are choosing by the way you are feeling. Enthusiasm brings greater enthusiasm. Be enthusiastic. Apathy and depression bring more of the same. Lift yourself out of these negative patterns and into the light of a new choice.

Choose your responses, thoughts, and actions, and live the life you really, really want to live.

Be conscious; choose wisely; stay present.

*I consciously choose
enthusiasm, joy, and love!
I am alive and awake in my skin.*

MYSTERY

Life is a journey into the mystery, the mystery and uncertainty of the unknown. It is a gradual opening and revealing of life's secrets. It is an amazing and delightful passage of days and years.

Life on Earth is a remarkable period of learning and living in the moment. Some moments simply pass by unnoticed; others are lived fully and intentionally. Most lives are lived somewhere in between.

Being present in the moment takes focus, intention, and determination. Serving others becomes one's joy. Overcoming the human is the ticket home to God.

Live the mystery with passion, love, and joy.

*Today I fearlessly embrace
the mystery
of my life on Earth.*

LIFE

Now that you are waking up, you understand that *you* are creating your reality. However, you still respond unconsciously to beliefs that you learned as a young child. It is time to become aware of what those beliefs are. You will find this quite enlightening. It will help you be aware of certain behaviors that you might prefer to change.

Each moment in life is a moment of choice.

Each moment is a time to choose what you really want.

Each moment is a new beginning.

Each moment is life now.

Each moment is life-giving.

Each moment can be life-changing.

Each moment is a pure sacred gift.

Open the gift of life and live it fully!

Thank You for the gift of life,
dear God,
and for the power to choose my response
to all this day may bring.

LIGHT

You are now remembering who you are and how much you love the Light. You trust Me, dear one, even while the human ego doubts. I trust you to be you, to live your essence fully, and to know your truth. You are a Divine Being of Light, having a human experience in classroom Earth. You are a being of love. Nothing else matters.

Today, surrender your fear of trusting Me. Live this trust. You yearn to go to the Light, to live in Love, Joy, and Beauty. You yearn to be home with Me and all the Heavenly helpers. With our help, you can know the light of your own being.

Be aware of your thoughts, which are the vehicle by which you create your world. You are both master and creator of your life. You bring either light or darkness into your experience. Create that which you want to live.

My Light is yours. I love you completely.

Living in the Light
I am happy, playful, and content.

SPIRITUAL PRACTICE

You ask what would help you most in your spiritual practice.

1. Be consistent. Meditate and pray and listen for My voice several times a day.

2. Be present. Contemplate in the Silence 30 minutes twice a day without computer, TV, or telephone interruptions. If your mind wanders, come back to the breath. Remember that practice makes perfect.

3. Stay in harmony and change your thoughts when you are out of sync with peacefulness.

4. Be grateful for whatever is before you in your life.

5. Use Me and the Angelic Host who are always with and around you. Love them. Use them!

6. Give service to others. Pray for them and help them in any way you can—run errands for them, talk to them, and encourage them on the phone.

7. Uplift others with your love. Allow them to feel safe with you by accepting them just the way they are.

*Today I make a recommitment
to my spiritual life.*

PERFECTION

When you give energy to something through your attention and feelings, you invite it into your world. Some things enhance your life with joy, expansion, love, and harmony. Other things, like the negativity of fear, doubt, and indecisiveness, bring disharmony and mis-creation. This is where you have work to do.

Use the law of forgiveness to rid your world of mis-creations. Life is easier as you overcome the human ego. That is what cleansing your world is all about. You give your power of creation away when, on autopilot or through unawareness, you choose the impulses of immediate gratification.

Decide to get your priorities straight. Choose perfection.

I am here to help you; just ask.

I am willing to correct
any mis-creation
and any imbalance in my life.
Help me, God.

BLESSING

Always bless others. Do not spend your time judging them. See them in My Light.

Blessing removes your focus from selfishness to caring for others.

Blessing connects you to your Divinity within.

Blessing brings inner joy to you and through you to the world.

Blessing brings you into the holiness of the present moment.

Blessing takes you out of your chattering mind and into purposeful action and usefulness.

Blessing energizes and refreshes your life!

BLESS! BLESS! BLESS!

This is a day of blessing.
I look upon everyone through the
eyes of God's Love.

REMEMBERING TRUTH

Remember who you are!

Remember that you are a living, breathing child of God.

Remember that your Divine Self is expanding in Light.

Remember that you are love.

Remember that you are here to serve.

Remember that you are never alone.

Remember that you are one with All that is.

Remember that I AM the life within you.

REMEMBER!

God,
help me remember my true nature today.
Help me to be all that You envision for me.

AWARENESS

BE PRESENT TODAY!

No matter what you are doing, be aware! It doesn't make any difference what the activity is; be fully present in it. Stop being a spectator; be an active participant in your life.

Your life is not a dress rehearsal; it is the real thing! Wake up and live. Fear, doubt, worry, and apathy disappear when life is lived with conscious awareness and full intention. Your energy flows with a true zest for living. Embrace your life! Live your life fully!

Be present today!

Moment to moment I am attentive,
awake, aware,
and actively participating in my life today.

TRUE COMFORT

At any moment you can choose to walk through the veil of your humanness and live in your Divinity. Then your service to others becomes one of love without human game playing. You play many games, and they keep you from being your true and real Self.

Game playing is an ego attempt to make you compete so you can be "better than" someone else, to acquire more things, or to judge and criticize. Another game you play is using food or other external things to comfort yourself. These are false comforters. Instead, you could talk to Me or switch your energy from self-absorption to serving others.

To receive guidance you must be present. Stop numbing out! Stop distracting yourself! Be here, now! Everything is NOW! There is no other place to be.

I AM with you. I AM everywhere.

Today I will be honest
about how I spend my time.

GUIDANCE

Use and follow My guidance always.

Use Me for everything.

Use Me instead of false comforters.

Use Me instead of numbness.

Use Me as your confidante.

Use Me to vent your anger and discover peace.

Use Me to spread love, laughter, compassion,
and hope.

Use Me to receive clarity.

Use Me to help you forgive.

Use Me to bless.

Use Me in every aspect of your life.

Use Me each and every now moment.

Use Me to remove any hidden doubt and fear.

Use Me as your mouth to speak, your eyes to see, your
ears to hear, and your heart to know.

Use Me to restore perfection in your life.

Use Me!

I know and trust that You are
here for me, God.
Your Presence offers everything I need.

CONNECTION

You yearn for a closer connection with Me. You yearn to feel My Presence and to stay in that awareness all through the day. You long to release the past so you can live fully in the now moment. There is no past! All is now! Everything in the Universe is NOW. Memories prevent the present from being experienced in the now moment. Stay present.

For awareness and connection to happen, meditate every day. Meditation takes you to a space of inner quiet where you can be free from outer noise.

Live each moment for the first time. No two moments are exactly the same. Use all your spiritual tools to perfect your world. I am here in the midst of life with you.

I AM with you always.

*Everyday moments are profound
when I stay connected to God.*

LIFE AND DEATH

You came into this lifetime to experience many different things. One of them was loss or perceived loss. You thought death was a real thing. You have learned that so-called *death* is an expansion of light.

The person who appears to die leaves the physical plane and resides then in a different plane or vibration. It is a higher vibration and humans cannot see those beings with their physical sight. That does not mean that those people who have gone before you do not live. They do.

Everything that exists is made of energy. Energy is manifested into material form in this world. When a person dies, it is only the physical body that stops breathing. The eternal essence of that person goes back into the unmanifested form or spirit.

It is quite simple, really. You are made of Light. And it is to the Light that you return.

Come home. Come and merge with Me in the Light.

Today I live in Light, I breathe the Light,
I bless the Light in all creation.

SILENCE

Beloved of My Heart,

Silence, meditation, and contemplation are means of inner renewal. Being still and allowing the mind to rest brings you into a deep sense of quiet. You move from *doing* to *being*. Give yourself permission to just BE.

You are beginning to understand the power of Silence. With conscious focus and intention, you direct your life energy to do its perfect work. From the Silence, the inner world, you project energy out into the world.

- Energy gathers in the Silence.

- Energy is directed from the Silence.

- Energy is conserved in the Silence.

- Energy expands and gains power in the Silence.

Remember to be still this day. Remember the power of the Silence within you.

I am still; I am quiet.
I direct my life energy from inner Stillness.
All is well in my world.

PRAYER

Dear One,

Hone your praying skills.

Any time that people, situations, projects, dreams of others, or health concerns come to your mind, *pray*. Anyone and anything that comes to your attention is yours to pray for.

Thy will be done.

May the Divine Plan be fulfilled.

May the Peace of God be with you.

These and similar phrases say it all. You do not need long prayers; short ones are perfect too. Keep practicing and you will feel more confident in praying.

When disasters happen in the world, simple words of faith and prayer will bring you comfort. Say, *I don't know what to pray for, God. You know what is needed. Thank you for helping. Please remove the fear in this situation and provide shelter, food, water, and relief. Thank you for answering.*

Remember, dear one, every prayer is heard and answered.

Today I hold the world in prayer.
I give every concern to God
and peace fills my heart.

DIVINE ORDER

All is in Divine Order in your world. Divine Order is moving, not stagnant, because it is always expanding. When My Order is in place, Light expands and Joy increases. Service is constant. Everyone is ready and willing to help everyone else. Cooperation is the norm. Happiness flows and expands. Divine Order is a place of ever-increasing beauty! Peace reigns supreme. Communication is telepathic with no way to misunderstand what is being said.

With Divine Order maintained, each human is free to explore and experience anything and everything. There is freedom to learn, make mistakes, learn again, and expand in the Light. Each experience leads to the next one. Each experience contributes to the tapestry of life in an individual, a nation, a world. This tapestry is a total of everything that has touched the life stream in any way.

Weave a joyful tapestry with your life today!

All is in Divine Order.

I live in the flow of Divine Order.
There is no need to struggle.
All can be peace if I allow it.

MISTAKES

Let us look at your fear of making mistakes. In this earthly life you *will* make mistakes. Everyone does. That is the nature of the human learning process. That is the way it is in this world. You have tools to correct those mistakes. Use them and be grateful.

For now you are unaware at times of just what needs correcting in your thoughts. Gradually you tune in and take corrective action. It is important for you to stay focused and rectify the mistakes whenever you are aware of them. All is coming to Perfection and that includes you, dear one.

Find the beauty, perfection, love, and joy when you are with others. Ask Me for help in returning to the Peace you long for in the midst of chaotic thinking, strong opinions, or gossip. Keep your mind free of negativity. You are the one in charge as the caretaker of your life.

Remember My guidance is always with you.

Today I make mistakes
and move right through them.
Nothing edges God out
in my thinking.

LOVE

Love!

Love like you have never loved before.

Love one another.

Love yourself.

Love your family.

Love your pets.

Love your friends.

Love your hobbies.

Love your perceived enemy.

Love Mother Earth.

Love Father Sky.

Love all beings, great and small.

Love all minerals.

Love all water.

Love and praise constantly.

Love beauty, flowers, sunrise, and sunset.

Love strangers.

Love your country.

Love every new moment.

Harm no one.

Forgive everyone.

Love!

Today I reflect the light of Heaven
everywhere I go.
I experience my world through the eyes
of love.

PRAYER

Let us talk about prayer. Prayer is more than the formulations you learn in religion. Those prayers are meant to be the beginning of your relationship with God. They establish the basis and habit of prayer.

Spontaneous prayer is what we are talking about now. Spontaneous prayer is that which comes from within your being at all times. It is your wonder and joy about life expressed with amazement and gratitude. Spontaneous prayer also comes when you are deeply concerned for someone else. You hold the person in the Light, asking for their highest good. Your prayer affirms that Divine Order is fulfilled in his or her life.

Spontaneous prayer accepts that all is here, now, and rejoices in this fullness. When things seem to be out of balance, ask that everything be realigned into balance and order.

Spontaneous prayer is a constant dialogue with Me, your Creator. It is talking to Me about *anything* and *everything* that comes to mind. It is claiming the joy and releasing the discomfort, talking about personal concerns and successes. It is asking for direction. It is communion.

Ask. I always answer.

May every breath and every heartbeat,
every thought and every action of this day
be a prayer.

SYNCHRONICITY

Synchronicity is everywhere around you.

Synchronicity is the reminder that all is in Divine Order, always and in all ways. Perhaps you have noticed how often things seem to come together in a miraculous way. At such a moment, everything fits together like fingers in a glove.

Synchronicity is the surprising fusion of seemingly different elements in any experience and in a short period of time. You manifest the parts with attention, thought, and feelings, even when you are unaware of calling them forth. The divergent parts and pieces fit together in a congruent whole; they are the perfect pieces to affirm, teach, or bring a different solution or direction to follow.

Synchronicity brings you surprise at its simplicity; wonder in how it all came together; joy in its affirmation.

Synchronicity is always a God-gift in a God-moment.

In gratitude I observe the delightful synchronicities that bless my life each day.

CHOICES

Keep on keeping on!

All is in Divine Timing; all is Divine Order. The human rebels against this and likes the status quo. This is a way to keep God out. Ego usurps power and claims it as its own. Ego likes to sabotage and does its best to do that in obvious or covert ways.

You are beginning to know when ego jumps in and makes life miserable for you.

Remember that you always have choices.

1. You may refuse to play ego's game.

2. You may "preach" to get attention without doing your work; that is called *talking the talk*.

3. You may choose to *walk the walk* and live from your spiritual nature to the best of your ability and willingness.

Life flows with grace and ease when ego is out of the way.

I am here with you and for you.

Use Me.

Let me walk in your power today, dear God.
Help me give attention only to Your guidance.
Keep me out of the shadow of ego and in
Your Light that never fails.

STILLNESS

Be still and know God. Be still and listen. Be still and just BE!

Remember who and what you are. Remember that your mission is to overcome the human ego and return home to Me. You are a Divine Being in embryo, remembering to live in love at all times.

Remember that your ego-self has no real power! Stop giving it energy. It is powerless on its own. It seems to have power when you focus on it, on its needs, feelings, and opinions. Then you feel some of those things as being real and that empowers ego.

Take your attention away from your mind-chatter, your endless ruminations, your likes and dislikes, and from your judgments of who is doing or not doing what. That is none of your business.

Give energy only to Me. Take care of your spiritual practice. Surrender to Me, give power to Me and to no one else. Live in peace, joy, happiness, laughter. Remember and know that I AM GOD.

I am with you always.

In the Stillness I remember my Divine Nature.
From the quiet of my soul I remember
God is my Source, my Life, my Everything.

GUIDANCE

Are you willing to meditate and receive a gentle guidance from within? Or do you prefer to be distracted and to put off the solutions that you seek? It is up to you. We are here to help you and We *do* help you. It happens quicker when you are willing to listen and follow through.

Do not get the wrong idea about this. Sometimes you need to sit in the Silence until you receive the guidance on how to proceed. Then there are other times when you are uncertain and not yet ready to take the next step. Through all this, guidance continues to unfold within you.

Clear direction comes when you are quiet. Meditation and contemplation give you the time and means needed to focus on the Divine. Clear your mind and renew yourself. Turn off your phones, TV, and computer; unplug from all distractions. In the Stillness allow the mystery of your life to unfold.

I quiet my mind.
I make room for the Divine Nature
of my being
to inform me.
Then I proceed in confidence.

AWARENESS

Be here, now!

You can have only one thought at a time. It seems that many thoughts flow through in a jumble, an entanglement of ideas, which are sometimes constructive and other times merely confusing and distracting.

By being present in the moment, you become aware of the chattering ego-mind, which uses energy to go in circles but thinks that it is actually doing something worthwhile. What it is really doing is creating unrest and disharmony within you.

Letting your mind chatter, without your controlling and monitoring it, creates unhappiness for you. This is what happens when the ego thinks it is in charge. But when ego becomes obedient to the inner Presence, you find peace and rest.

Choose harmony, dear one.

Choose peace.

*I take charge of my life today
by embracing the moment and
disengaging from disruptive thoughts.*

POWER

You are at another turning point in your commitment to doing your inner work. Are you ready to jump in or get out? It is up to you. We are here to help you, but you must choose to receive the help. You choose each and every moment. Make choices that fulfill your inner yearning.

Give no power to negative things.

Give no power to habits that keep you stuck.

Give no power to compulsions.

Give no power to your human ego.

Live in the Light of day and remove the shadows.

Give power to the Light.

Give power to serving others.

Give power to having fun.

Give power to laughing, dancing, singing, playing.

Give power to happiness, joy, and contentment.

Give power to God alone.

I am fully committed to my spiritual path.
I release patterns of laziness and distraction.
I give power to being light-hearted
and God-focused.

SILENCE

Allow your life to unfold in its perfection. Focus on Me, your Presence, as the only guiding light in you. Stop focusing on the opinions, gossip, and criticisms of other people. All of that colors your world with negativity. Give no power to human creation. Study, contemplate, and remember in the Silence.

The Silence is your friend and your teacher. Revelations, answers, and solutions are gifts of the Silence. Peace flows to you in the Silence.

The Silence encourages you to be quiet and calm. There, in the Silence, you spend time with yourself only. You watch your thoughts; you become aware of what to focus your attention on.

Climb into the Silence and stay there.

Melt into the Silence.

I AM there.

Today I remember that Silence is my friend.
It brings me rest from the outer world
while it centers me in my
inner sanctuary.

PRESENCE

Who you think you are is what you are. Being that is your goal. As you ask for help, you expand in Light, beingness, and freedom. There is nothing else to do and nowhere else to go.

Although you think there is much to accomplish, there is only expansion of Light, Love, Kindness, Service to others and, incidentally, to yourself. Each act of kindness fills the world with more kindness.

As you allow love to flow, you find that you do not have to be concerned with the so-called *past* which is non-existent in the present, known as NOW. The past is only a memory that surfaces, and it has no power of its own. It only has the power you give to it.

The effects of your every thought and of each action are everywhere, because all is one and one is all. Do you understand? It does not matter how big or small each thought or action is; it influences everything.

Be aware.

Be awake.

Be consciously present NOW.

I am present. I am loving.
Each moment I expand into greater Light
and greater service.

SELF-KNOWLEDGE

There are many questions that will surface for you on your spiritual path. Here are a few to contemplate:

- What do you want to know, understand, be, and do in this life?

- Is your commitment to your soul's path based on words or deeds?

- What are you willing to do or to change in order to stay focused on your spiritual goals?

- Do you give for the joy of giving or merely out of duty?

- Are you God-focused in your life or ego-driven?

- In what ways are you serving others and giving back to Creation?

Take these questions into the Silence often. The answers will be revealing to you and will help you make good choices.

Always be true to yourself and your inner knowing.

In the Silence I ask myself difficult questions.
The answers I hear guide me to
good choices and right action.
I listen and follow.

TRUST

Trust is a life lesson for you, as it is for many. You are learning to discriminate between what is worthy of your trust and what is not. People sometimes try to gain power and control through misrepresentations such as scams, false promises, and lies. Discrimination will warn you that something is not right. Ask Me for help in making the distinction and then trust your instincts.

Trust is a matter of surrender and then knowing that you are taken care of. Everything that you really need is waiting for you. Claim the things you need and want.

Trusting gives you the willingness to let all of Heaven help you. You do not have to do everything by yourself. Trusting that you are safe and that you are okay, you let go and ask for help. You trust that you will receive, and you always do.

Freedom comes through trusting the good. Trust is a reward for surrendering. Trust and surrender are part of a holy continuum. The greater the trust, the stronger the surrender and the greater still the Peace that is within you.

I trust that Divine Order is present in all things.
I surrender to the good of God's bounty.
Peace and freedom are my reward.

SPIRITUAL GROWTH

Take charge of your spiritual life.

- Talk to Me and your unseen guides and helpers constantly.

- Hold the mental picture of what you want to manifest in your world and then fearlessly embrace it.

- Give no power to anything that prevents the fulfillment of your divine plan.

- Love Me with every thought, breath, word, and action.

- Meditate in the silence.

- Pray and decree from your inner sanctuary.

- Take your inner peace into the outer world.

- Melt into the Silence. Just Be with Me.

- Take pleasure in time with family and friends.

- Find and live your passion.

ENJOY LIFE FULLY!

Day by day I grow in spiritual wisdom.
Step by step I walk the path to God.

JOY

My Dear One,

The Power and Love of the Universe reveals itself to you in unexpected, truth-filled moments. As you trust Me, you keep feeling the joy and freedom of beingness.

There is nothing to do and nowhere to go. It is all here now. Whatever you do and wherever you go, it is all already here now.

Be aware how open your heart chakra is. Notice the warmth and peace you feel. Words do not and cannot capture your expansion and joy.

The word "trust" today is just a word. Your fear of trusting Me is gone. It has never been. Your feelings are clear; no hooks of doubt remain for you to use. Rejoice, dear one; this gift is yours because you have prayed to be unmasked and totally open with Me.

You are living in joyful amazement. This is another step you have taken. Rejoice, laugh, praise, play. Delight in this day. Trust Me.

God of my being,
I trust You!
I trust You in every aspect of my life.

RELATIONSHIPS

Every relationship that you have is with yourself. You have a relationship with everything upon which you focus, think, and feel. A relationship is an interaction between two things—animate or inanimate, materialized or imagined, objects apparent or not apparent.

You have a relationship with air as you breathe it, with thought as you think it. You have a relationship with people, animals, plants, and minerals as you encounter them. And you also have relationships with ideas, feelings, and with numbness.

Your relationship with Me, your God, is based on the perception you hold within yourself of Me. Your relationships with people in your life are built the same way. The difference is that each person makes individual choices in molding and changing those relationships.

Every relationship allows you the opportunity to fine-tune your skills in being harmonious, present, loving, faithful, open, and honest. You perfect yourself when you choose how you are, and what you will or will not accept in each relationship.

All life is an ongoing relationship.
Today I am aware of how I relate to others.
I choose harmony in all situations.

DIVINE ORDER

All is in Divine Order. Nothing happens by chance, accident, or mistake, even though it may appear that way. Everything is the energy of creation. Energy comes where it is called. Be aware of what you create; be aware of what you are calling into your life. Creation can be amazingly magnificent or equally troublesome.

Human order is not the same as Divine Order. Human order often creates pain and chaos. It brings lessons and experiences that individuals need to walk through in this lifetime. Human order, or disorder, seems to bring stress, war, anger, isolation, hatred, lack, discomfort, fear, and no cooperation with others. This leads to power-grabbing and more world discontent.

Divine Order brings healing, cooperation, solutions, and helpful new ways to be and think. Divine Order is always love, Light, and blessing. It gives individuals opportunities to discover who they are and to accomplish that for which they embodied.

Divine Order is a balance of energy and brings peace, harmony, joy, and love.

I trust in the Divine Order
that governs all life.
In this trust my life flows with joy and peace.

HEALING

When you hear anyone talking in a complaining way and saying things that are less than positive, stop participating! Transform the negative immediately into something neutral. Be the Presence that nullifies the negativity right now, so that it cannot affect you or any other part of life.

Be clear about this—you are not to take part in fault-finding, criticizing, judging, or condoning harmful actions.

Opportunities to participate in the tearing down of others occur everywhere. Keep your guard up. Ask for My protection. Feel it always with you. Feel as if you are transmuting the negative until it is consumed and removed.

Stay awake and aware.

Angels are here to help you.

Today I keep my mind clear of negativity.
I affirm the good in everyone and
join in the healing of the world.

INVITATIONS

Live from perfection and then all things that are not perfection will fall away. Face your tendency to isolate yourself from others. When someone invites you to join them in doing something, be gracious in accepting. Do not be ambivalent. Ask yourself what the resistance to joining with others is really about.

Accepting invitations to interact with others keeps those invitations coming. Refusing invitations tells other people that you do not want to be with them or that you are not interested in what they are doing. See each invitation as an opportunity to learn and grow.

Allow life to flow through you. Take advantage of the many opportunities that life offers you. Be alive in your skin and awake in your mind and soul!

Happy surprises await me in interacting with others.
I say "yes" to the invitations that come my way.
I embrace life more fully by opening to new experiences and possibilities.

AWARENESS

Stop and smell the roses of your life. Be aware of all the things that give you joy, like the sunrise, the beauty of nature, the sounds of life on Earth. Savor the moment and revel in the gifts that are given to you each instant. Look for the gifts all around you; find them; stay present in the *presents* of the day.

Be in the moment, each moment, and watch it unfold. There is nowhere else to go and nothing else to do. Be! In the quiet, allow life to flow before your eyes. Find the gifts waiting to be discovered. Accept the new gift that each moment brings.

Rejoice and delight in unexpected revelations and unfolding surprises. Simple pleasures fill your senses; seeing a hummingbird, the beauty of a flower, the fullness of a tree's canopy, a squirrel swinging on a limb. Family, pets, and friends are a few things that give you joy, gratitude, and appreciation for life.

Everywhere around me the world blesses my senses with beauty and wonder.
I stay present to the simplicity and mystery of each unfolding moment.

INNER POWER

You are often confused about the meaning of the word *power* and are uncertain about its use. Power, rightly understood, is the use of love and life energy directed to accomplish a specific purpose. This is the power that created the universe, planets, and everything that is. This power is unfathomable to the human mind, because it is always constructive and utilized for the good of all.

Power, as used by the ego alone, is corrupt. In business and government it can often be the norm to manipulate and intimidate others with lies and cover-ups. Individual gain becomes the primary selfish goal.

Inner power is My gift to you and it is a necessity. You experience it as the determination to be all that you can be. It means loving Me, your Divine Presence, with every fiber of your being. Inner power propels you to correct your human mistakes by forgiving them and changing the habits and patterns that impede your growth.

Do not be afraid of the power I have given you. Use it to create the world of your dreams.

*Today I embrace the power of creation
given to me by God.
I consciously create the life I really want
to live.*

DISCOVERY

It is the small things that make a difference. See the small things of life as the true gifts they are. See the quirks of nature that add variety to life. Notice the unpredictability of your human nature—its emotions, its joys, its compassion, as well as its inconsistencies. All these things make the world a surprise. Embrace the great diversity of life with a smile, a simple acknowledgment of wonder.

Do not judge whether things are good or bad. Allow life to unfold and see how you feel living in the world of discovery. Nothing is ever the same, although it seems to be. Find the treasure in each moment. There is much to discover. With a positive perspective you see everything differently. Each moment is a lifetime experience.

I embrace the wonder of life
and allow myself to be
delighted, surprised, and blessed.

SELF-LOVE

You have often heard the instruction to serve others and to love and help others. There is one thing missing in that formula. You must love, serve, support, and be there for yourself *first* before you can possibly be there for others. This does not mean to forget or ignore them; it means to practice and learn the skills of self-love. Then you are ready to love and serve those I send to you.

Be gentle with yourself; then you can be gentle with everyone else. Feed yourself with love and in the quantities that your body requires; then you have the physical strength to nurture others. Be kind to yourself; then kindness flows from you in appropriate ways.

Love yourself and minister to yourself because your life matters!

*I am kind and gentle with myself today.
I treat self and all others with
compassion and love.*

LOVE

Stand in Me; Stand in Love and ignore everything else. Cling to Me no matter what is happening around you. Outer appearances often seem frightening and overwhelming to your human mind. When you cling to Me and live by inner guidance and direction, you find and live your freedom.

Stand with Me; I will help you perfect your world. The world of human beings is often filled with negativity and fear. Much of the energy on planet Earth is heavy and oppressive. It is the heaviness of doubt, worry, fear, judgment, anger, criticism and other ego-driven thoughts and emotions.

Remember that you are a being of love. Love raises the energy within and around you; your fears are removed and joy returns to your awareness. Love is the promise of new beginnings in each moment of time.

Seriousness gets some things done.
Joy makes activities more fun.
And love gives all things new meaning.

VIGILANCE

Your word for today is "simplify." Simplify your thoughts; simplify your spoken words; simplify everything. Keep all that you do or think smoothly flowing, easy, uncomplicated, and direct. Use simple sentences, basic ideas, and unembellished language. Keep the modifiers unadorned. Use direct and basic statements. Be clear in what you think, say, and do.

You control what you think at all times. Be aware of your thoughts and the resulting actions. Choose consciously what you think and what you are creating and manifesting in your world.

Stop playing ego games; stop trying to use manipulation to get what you want. Say what you mean and mean what you say! This is the way to simplify your words.

Simplify your environment too. De-clutter and organize. Organization is also simple, yet it takes perseverance and a change of your habits. Simplify your life and let all be in Divine Order.

Today I am vigilant over my thoughts.
I am honest and direct with my
spoken words.
My actions come from clarity and integrity.

COOPERATION

Cooperation is the word of the day. Cooperation means working together for the common good. Cooperate with others in designing the easiest and best way to do something, to accomplish a mutual goal, to find a solution to a problem. Cooperation builds love, respect, acceptance, and humor. Cooperating with one another expands each one's understanding and knowledge of others.

Through cooperation, new ways of doing things emerge. Often quicker and easier solutions can be found that support your lives. Friendships form out of this new unity and the world becomes a better place. The world needs and is now demanding greater harmony between people, countries, and families— everyone, everywhere.

Cooperate with Mother Earth. Take care of your planet, your physical home. Stop the pollution, the wars, and the waste. Stop taking advantage of each other and the resources of the earth. Restore; recycle; repair. Be your brother's keeper. Love each other; cooperate with one another; bless and serve the whole of creation.

*I serve the good of all
through conscious cooperation.
I am a blessing by living in harmonious
collaboration with others.*

CHOICE

You, dear one, have all the tools to create the world you ideally want to live in. Be conscious of what you are doing. *You* have created the world you are presently living in. When something fills you with joy and love, choose more of it. When something displeases you, choose again. Everything is a choice.

Today you are consciously choosing the thoughts, feelings, and words that make you joyful. You are aware. In awareness you remember that you always have choices and that you must choose something. Choose wisely.

Ask yourself if each choice is leading you to the good you seek or the results you desire. If not, choose something that serves you better. Hold in mind what you really want and then make wise choices that bring form to your thoughts.

You, dear one, are divine. Create from and in your divinity. Create positive, up-beat results. Give yourself permission to be fully you. Dream big; manifest those dreams and possibilities. Expand your light and increase your vibration. The choice is always yours.

I choose wisely. I choose consciously.
And my choices create a world
of wonder and joy for myself and others!

RELATIONSHIPS

Let us speak more about relationships. The only way to develop, expand, and enjoy a relationship is to make it a priority. Put your focus and energy into it. Give it attention. Look for and find the love, joy, and perfection in it. The more you focus on those positive qualities, the more often you will see them.

As you examine each relationship, you will find differences. No two are alike. You are different in each one. Your perceived wants, desires, and satisfaction vary from moment to moment and play out in your interactions with others. When you are unaware, you are having a relationship just within yourself.

This brings us back to an important question: *What do you really want in each relationship?* Once you determine this, ask yourself what you are willing to do in order to manifest that ideal right now.

Relationships are the heart of my life.
Because they are so important, I lovingly
give them the attention they need to thrive.

PERFECTION

Remember that each moment is a gift. Find the "present" each moment brings and embrace it. Dialogue with each gift to discover how you might use it in your life. Accept the gift and follow through on using it.

Watch your life expand into the perfection of the moment. Praise, thank, and bless each moment, each expansion—each and every gift.

You are the creator of your world. Create beauty, joy, fun, and perfection each day. It is as easy to create perfection as it is to create imperfection. Create consciously, in awareness. Monitor your thoughts. Allow constructive and uplifting thoughts. Pay no attention to anything else.

Each moment I wait for your return to Me. Do your work and come home to Me; come home to where the human is always obedient to the Light.

As I am present in each new moment of life
I feel my connection with You, dear God,
and with all that You would have me be,
know, see, and understand.

DIVINE ORDER

Dear Beloved One,

ALL IS IN DIVINE ORDER!

You trust Me more now than you have in a long time. How does that feel? Do you know that you are surrounded, enveloped, and clothed in My Love every moment? There is nothing else to know. Remembering My Love brings you insights and the certainty you seek. You are surrendering more every day and allowing this Love to fill and direct you. You are never alone and can never be alone.

Ask Me for help when you want or need clarity, illumination, and guidance. Let Me be your knowing, your eyes, ears, thoughts, words, feelings, and understanding. I AM THE ALL IN ALL. I AM everywhere, always, the known and the unknown, the hidden and revealed.

I AM.

I surrender.
I fall into the mystery of my life,
trusting that God is present always.
All is in Divine Order.

BEAUTY

Allow your spirit to unfold and to blossom. Bring your gifts and talents to play in each new day of life. Pay attention to what you are planting through your thoughts, words, actions, feelings, and choices.

If you plant a flower garden and watch the flowers bloom and grow, you notice how they expand. You are doing the same in the Light of My Love for you. You are like the fragile flower that gives everything it is to the world without holding anything back. Its beauty continues to expand; the air is filled with its fragrance and joy of being. That is what you are and what you are allowing yourself to be.

Be the Light that you are! Be all that you came here to be!

My life is a garden in which I plant the seeds of Divine beauty through my thoughts, words, and actions.

CHOICES

Release! Surrender! Allow! Be!

You have nothing to do nor anywhere to be except *here*, *now*. Allow the day to simply and easily unfold. Stop living in lists of things to do. Stay in the moment! Each moment unfolds before you with infinite possibilities. Life unfolds moment by moment and choice by choice. Choose the world you desire to live in and create it by your choices.

There are infinite choices to make as you begin each day. What are you choosing? Do you know? Are you aware? Being conscious, you know what you are creating. Being lazy and numb, you do not even know what your choices are.

Monitor your thoughts and actions. Ask yourself if what you are doing, thinking, or being is creating the world you really want. Does this feel good or not? Is this choice for the highest good for you, the universe, or your family?

Choose wisely each moment. Live in knowing awareness.

Yours is the wisdom with which I choose my actions today, dear God.
You are the Love and the Joy
I carry with me into each interaction with others.

LOVE

Love and bless everything and everyone! You question this directive only when you see the evil that people can heap upon each other and this world. You must learn to look beyond appearances and see with new eyes.

Love the Perfection within all, the Light and Love from which creation comes. Give no power to the negative consequences which result from the choices of the human ego alone. Remove the power you have given the ego and all its judgments. Stop investing in limitation and fear. Those are the means through which the ego thrives and brings destructive patterns to the world.

People who act insanely and harm others have a spark of Divinity within them too. That God Self within them is what you are to love, speak to, and bless with your prayers.

Love the Divine perfection within each person whether it is visible to you or not. When you love others, you bring Love into your own life. Love is the perfection you yearn for and Peace is always the gift of that Love.

Love is all I seek today,
and Love is all I find.

BALANCE

Bring balance into all areas of your life. Bring balance into all that you do each day, your service to others, your care of yourself and your family. Make the necessary choices to have balance in your fiscal responsibilities, in your work life and your time of rest, and in recreation and quiet.

Bring balance into your use of technology and of other things that can distract you from being fully present. How you use the technological toys and gadgets of the world determines your level of awareness.

Balance is most quickly established by stepping back from your activities for a moment. See what you are really doing. Invite the guidance of Spirit to help you bring peace and harmony into your life. Choose where you will put your energy. Be aware of what you are doing and then all energy is returned to Source and balanced out.

Stay awake and be focused! Stay awake and be focused every moment.

Thank you, God,
for showing me that the things which seem
wrong or out of balance in my outer world
today
are just a reflection of what needs to shift
within me.

LIFE

Life is what you make of it; it is all your choice. How you view life is what you create it to be. Yes, you truly create your Heaven on Earth, or anything else, by your feelings, thoughts, words, actions, beliefs, habits, and choices. You create your happiness or unhappiness. You choose your values and then live them to the best of your ability.

You help heal and perfect the world with your actions, thoughts, decrees, and prayers. They all carry the power of creation. Hold the focus of perfection and be the instrument of Peace, Love, and Forgiveness.

Use your power to manifest the world you really want. Be like a radio station and broadcast harmony, freedom, blessing, and abundance to the world. You can do this. You can do this easily and it *will* bring results.

Play, laugh, sing, and dance your way through life.

Make your life fun!

I love and appreciate the gift of life.
All the choices I am making shape my life
each and every day.

INTEGRITY

It is time to pick up the pace of your expansion into the Light. Be intentional and aware of your thoughts. Stop living in negativity and doubt. Live your faith instead. Take a leap of faith each moment; trust and follow your inner guidance.

It is time to release excuses! Of themselves, excuses have no power. You give them all the power and meaning you want them to have. Excuses keep you stuck in a rut; they stop the flow of My grace in your life. They are always ego-driven and are intended to keep you from your potential.

Excuses produce guilt and keep you in your self-made prison. Excuses keep you "little" and stop the light from expanding within you. Excuses are false and are not relevant. They keep you living in the past or future, rather than in the present moment. Excuses sabotage your spiritual growth and keep you on the cycle of birth and death.

Say what you mean, do what you say, live fully and truthfully. Give up the crutch of your excuses now. Forgive yourself. Create your days wisely by living from the Divine Power within, taking responsibility for your every thought, word, and action.

*I give up all excuses today
and live in full spiritual integrity.*

FREEDOM

Savor your freedom. Freedom for you is freedom from the creations of the ego. Be vigilant and transmute ego-thoughts as quickly as you are aware of creating them. You thought your ego was necessary and that it helped you to survive when you forgot your oneness with Me. Ego was your best coping tool and your "friend." Now ego expects and demands that *its* advice be followed. The more you listen to and follow your ego, the more distant you feel from Me.

You have empowered your ego all your life. It seemed to be the only thing you could count on to walk with you through all your days on Earth. You forgot all about Me; you felt unsafe even thinking about Me. You believed that I had abandoned you. Separation became your reality and the source of much misery.

Today you know Me and trust My perfect care for you. You yearn to be with Me permanently, without any distractions. Come home to Me, dear one, in joyful acceptance of My Love.

With an open heart and trusting mind
I accept God's love for me today.
I listen only to His Voice within me.

FORGIVENESS

Forgive constantly. Ask Me to help you and I will. Know that you are in charge of your thoughts always. Monitor your thoughts, feelings, words, and actions. Be aware of each imperfection, each limited thought that causes you to judge or criticize self or others. Forgive each negative thought and watch your world change.

Your forgiveness consumes any mis-creation and replaces that emptiness with love and peace. Insist that perfection fill you and your world. Forgive everything that is less than holy. Use My love to consume all mis-creation.

Forgive yourself when you forget your true nature, when you get lazy and want to numb out, when you procrastinate and forget to be present and live your life from the highest that is within you.

Forgive each and every tendency to think of yourself as small, insignificant, or unworthy of My love.

Come back to Me in forgiveness. Stay with Me in each and every loving thought. Let forgiveness be your daily path.

As I forgive, I am free to love again.

SPIRITUAL PRACTICE

Unite with Me daily through your spiritual practice.

- Live in your Divinity.

- Serve with love and joy always.

- Bless everyone and wish the best for them.

- Be kind and gentle to all.

- Talk to Me; use Me; live My Way.

- Surrender all your preconceived ideas, your procrastination, your rebellion, and your excuses.

- Live each moment fully.

- Be here NOW.

- Love, Bless, Forgive.

Today, dear God, I surrender all and
I live in Your love and light.
Help me feel Your Presence always.

PRAYER TO THE DIVINE PRESENCE WITHIN

Dear Beloved I AM Presence, God of My being,

Thank You for illumination and inner knowing. I rejoice in Your love, light, and instruction. Thank You for all the "aha" moments in My life. I am reveling in knowing that there is no "outer" world. What seems like the outer is but a reflection of my inner world showing Me things within Myself that need attention. Whenever I judge or criticize anything, I am seeing a part of me that needs love and forgiveness.

Thank You for direction. Thank You for lighting my way to being, seeing, and knowing. I celebrate life and living. Today I choose to be proactive and live with love, passion, and enthusiasm. Whatever I choose, I manifest in my world.

Thank You, dear Presence, for showing me ways to be joyful and to serve with passion. Thank you for showing me the difference between just existing and living life fully.

Keep this awareness sustained within me, oh God.

In and with You I am always safe, and I am alive forever.

Amen.

ACKNOWLEDGMENTS

This book is a gift of my Creator Self, which I call my *I AM* Presence, and affirms my spiritual journey. I am influenced by the teachings of Judaism (my religion of birth), the I AM teachings of the Saint Germain press, and concepts of other religions. I feel like an Essene, a secluded Jewish sect that lived before the birth of Jesus and studied all the contemporary writings, knowledge, and wisdom that they could find. I have followed a similar path in coming home to God.

This book would not have been written without the support and dedication of Louise Dunn, my editor, co-writer, and spiritual mentor. Her love, expertise, support, and encouragement made the concepts flow in power and understanding.

I am also grateful for the encouragement of friends who read some of the entries in this book and offered me further clarity. I thank my family for their continued support of whatever I choose to do in life and their encouragement that I follow my heart's guidance. You are my life's joy and gift.

CPSIA information can be obtained at www.ICGtesting.com
Printed in the USA
267880BV00006B/10/P